T0132396

I Am Magical
Yo Soy Mágico

Written by Karina Jacob

Illustrated by Victoria Bruno

Copyright © 2017 Karina Jacob.

All rights reserved. No part of this book may be used or reproduced by any means, graphic, electronic, or mechanical, including photocopying, recording, taping or by any information storage retrieval system without the written permission of the author except in the case of brief quotations embodied in critical articles and reviews.

Balboa Press books may be ordered through booksellers or by contacting:

Balboa Press
A Division of Hay House
1663 Liberty Drive
Bloomington, IN 47403
www.balboapress.com
844-682-1282

Because of the dynamic nature of the Internet, any web addresses or links contained in this book may have changed since publication and may no longer be valid. The views expressed in this work are solely those of the author and do not necessarily reflect the views of the publisher, and the publisher hereby disclaims any responsibility for them.

Any people depicted in stock imagery provided by Getty Images are models, and such images are being used for illustrative purposes only.
Certain stock imagery © Getty Images.

Illustrated by: Victoria Bruno

ISBN: 978-1-5043-7282-4 (sc)
ISBN: 978-1-5043-7281-7 (e)

Print information available on the last page.

Balboa Press rev. date: 10/21/2020

I Am Magical
Yo Soy Mágico

Through my journey of spiritual exploration, I felt inspired to write "I Am Magical," a children's book about self-awareness. By sharing this experience with children, this book intends to light a little flame in their hearts and minds, to make a better world. It is a simple, fun, and uplifting bilingual book to enjoy with the whole family.

The following idea is in the content of the book:

Be the magical energy of change to make the difference you wish to see in the world. It's like the analogy of the mirror; you have to be magical with a smile first so the mirror [of life] can reflect the magic of that smile back to you.

I am grateful for the loving support and encouragement of my family, friends, and teachers. I also want to thank Victoria for all her beautiful illustrations that make this book shine with love and talent.

♥ ♥ ♥

A través de mi camino de exploración espiritual, me sentí inspirada a escribir "Yo Soy Mágico", un libro para niños sobre la conciencia de uno mismo. Al compartir esta experiencia con los niños, este libro intenta encender una pequeña llama en sus corazones y en sus mentes, para lograr un mundo mejor. Este es un libro bilingüe, simple, divertido y que eleva el espíritu, para disfrutarlo con la familia.

La siguiente idea está en el contenido del libro:

Sé la energía mágica del cambio para hacer la diferencia que tú deseas ver en el mundo. Es como la analogía del espejo; tú tienes que ser mágico y sonreír primero, para que el espejo [de la vida] pueda reflejarte la magia de esa sonrisa.

Estoy agradecida por el amor, apoyo y aliento de mi familia, amigos y maestros. También agradezco a Victoria por sus hermosas ilustraciones que hacen que este libro brille con amor y talento.

When I choose to be magical,

Cuando yo elijo ser mágico,

wonderful things happen...

pasan cosas maravillosas...

I greet and say Hi!

Yo saludo y digo ¡Hola!

Others greet and say Hi! just like me.

Otros saludan y dicen ¡Hola! así como yo.

I am happy and smile.

Yo soy feliz y sonrío.

Others are happy and smile, just like me.

Otros son felices y sonríen, así como yo.

I love and hug.

Yo amo y abrazo.

Others love and hug, just like me.

Otros aman y abrazan, así como yo.

I sing and dance.

Yo canto y bailo.

Others sing and dance, just like me.

Otros cantan y bailan, así como yo.

I play and share.

Yo juego y comparto.

Others play and share, just like me.

Otros juegan y comparten, así como yo.

I am quiet, I breathe, and I am at peace.

Yo estoy en silencio, respiro y estoy en paz.

Others are quiet, they breathe, and they are at peace, just like me.

Otros están en silencio, respiran y están en paz, así como yo.

Beautiful things happen when...

¡Lindas cosas pasan cuando ...

I choose to be magical!

yo elijo ser mágico!

I have to be magical first so others can reflect, like a mirror, the magic back to me!

¡Yo tengo que ser mágico primero para que otros
me puedan reflejar la magia como un espejo!

No matter who or where you are...

¡Sin importar quién eres o dónde estés...

you can choose to be magical

tú puedes elegir ser mágico

and the world becomes magical too!

y el mundo se vuelve mágico también!

Karina Jacob, Author
Karina was born and raised in Asunción, Paraguay, which inspired her to write in English and Spanish. She is an early childhood educator and believes in the love that each one of us have in our hearts, and when we share it with others, we make the world a better place.

Karina nació y creció en Asunción, Paraguay, lo cual le inspiró a escribir en inglés y español. Ella es maestra de párvulos y cree en el amor que cada uno de nosotros tiene en el corazón, y cuando lo compartimos con los demás, hacemos que el mundo sea mejor.

Victoria Bruno, Illustrator

Victoria was born and raised in Santiago, Chile. A self-taught artist, she is an early childhood educator that loves to teach and create. She believes in freedom and mutual love. She dreams of a world full of colors where everyone can see their reflection in each other.

Victoria nació y creció en Santiago, Chile. Es una artista autodidacta y maestra de párvulos, que adora enseñar y crear. Ella cree en la libertad y el amor mutuo. Sueña con un mundo lleno de colores donde todos puedan verse reflejados en el otro.

ENDORSEMENT

This book is magical because it lifts your heart and shares with delight one of the simple and most powerful truths of life. Thank you Karina for this gift to all children and the child in us all.

– Rev. David McArthur, author Your Spiritual Heart

This beautifully illustrated book invites us in to share the magical world of children. Together, we are encouraged to reflect with delight the beauty we see in the world and BE MAGICAL!

Karina, I look forward to reading your books to my grandson. Thank you for sharing your creation with me. I feel honored to witness its birth!

– Carolyn Janson–Educator, Grandmother and licensed HeartMath trainer and coach

Printed in the United States
By Bookmasters